Slow Reading

Slow Reading

By John Miedema

Litwin Books, LLC
Duluth, Minnesota

Published in 2009

Published by Litwin Books, LLC
P.O. Box 3320
Duluth, MN 55803
http://litwinbooks.com/

This book is printed on acid-free paper that meets present
ANSI standards for archival preservation.

Cover photo by C. Ekholm Photography

Library of Congress Cataloging-in-Publication Data

Miedema, John.
 Slow reading / by John Miedema.
     p. cm.
 Summary: "A study of voluntary slow reading from diverse an-
gles"--Provided by publisher.
 Includes bibliographical references and index.
 ISBN 978-0-9802004-4-7 (acid-free paper)
 1. Books and reading. 2. Reading. I. Title.
 Z1003.M58 2009
 028'.9--dc22
                                        2008054742

For Kraemer, Samantha, and for my wife, Sue

Contents

Acknowledgments

The author gratefully acknowledges the guidance, suggestions and support of a number of people. Dr. Lynne McKechnie supervised my independent research on slow reading, performed as part of the course requirements for a Master of Library and Information Science at the University of Western Ontario. I am grateful to Rory Litwin for giving slow reading a second wind by suggesting I expand my research into this book. Thanks to Holly Cole for inviting me to speak at the Thinking Ahead Symposium at the Salt Lake City Public Library; it was helpful to talk with a crowd about slow reading. The writing of this book has benefitted from the contributions of a number of visitors to my website. I would like to give special acknowledgement for the comments and support of Scott Condon, Walt Crawford, Jason Hammond, Jim Murdoch, Pete Smith, Peter Stephens, and Jessamyn West. I am delighted that C. Ekholm agreed to the use of her photo on the cover.

Preamble and Overview

Slow reading is about reading at a reflective pace. The idea of reading more slowly may seem odd in a time of increasing demand for speed reading of volumes of information. Certainly, it is often important to be able to read quickly. Those who read slowly by nature only admit to it reluctantly. I am a slow reader. A book that takes me a month to read others might consume in a weekend. Slow reading is sometimes considered to reflect slow thinking, and I do not object to that association. Reading a book slowly allows for a deeper relationship with stories and ideas. When I read a book slowly it continues to influence me even years later.

For the past two years I have followed the formal research and informal web dialogue on slow reading. There are some consistent themes. In general, slow reading is regarded as a negative thing because it is perceived to be an involuntary condition. Research on slow reading is almost exclusively about physical barriers to reading such as dyslexia and eye disorders. Clearly, in these cases, slow reading is a problem and interventions may be appropriate to increase reading speed. However, one also hears of students forced to read long or difficult books and complaining about being slow readers. These students are targeted by vendors of speed reading courses. For a price, a student can learn to break the bad habits that cause slow reading. Implicit is the assumption that slow reading is not involuntary but can be cured by learning the right techniques. These students might share my resistance to rushing a good book; it feels like a violation of the author's intent and my own need to process it properly. An increasing number of people are get-

ting frustrated with information overload and are choosing
to read slowly. They share a conviction that slow reading is
an advantage, a pleasure when reading fiction and an aid to
comprehension when deciphering a complex text.

As part of a Master of Library and Information Science
degree, I undertook an independent study to gather research on the voluntary practice of slow reading. I posted
the results on my website. Rory Litwin, publisher of Litwin
Books, suggested turning the research into a book. This invi-
tation was a pleasant turn for me, but it was also a good idea
for another reason. The independent research was a part of
a graduate course, and its time demands forced a contradic-
tion with the subject matter. For much of the original research on slow reading I relied heavily on speed reading
techniques. I had to admit that in some contexts, I am a fast
reader. In fact, I work in information technology and can
read my own code faster than other eyes can follow. I
thought of myself as a slow reader only because I did not
count these other practices as reading. For this book, I had
the opportunity to reread the source material more slowly
and carefully. Still, there were many cases in which the material did not require or deserve slow reading. This fact rein-
forces an important theme that slow reading is not always
about reading as slow as possible. A slow reader might skim
a book, only slowing down for the good parts. Slow reading
is a voluntary practice taking many different forms.

This book is a meditation on the many meanings of slow
reading. It is organized into four essays, each making many
passing references to other sources in the hope that this
book serves a bibliographic function for others interested in
research on slow reading. Each essay draws on the research
and ideas and offers an original perspective. The first essay,
"The Personal Nature of Slow Reading", traces the practice

of slow reading back to the symbolic eating of books by prophets in the Bible. Later on, the technique of close reading was adopted by scholars as a way to extract the many layers of meaning from a complex text. Close reading became associated with scholarly analysis, but modern educators find that slow reading techniques are useful for teaching reading skills to students even of young ages. Personal control over the rate and content of reading is essential to the enjoyment of reading, which in turn creates lifelong readers. The accelerating quantity of reading materials available today increases the likelihood that the right book exists for any reader's given needs, though it also increases the challenge of finding it.

The second essay, "Slow Reading in an Information Ecology" examines how the traditional practice of reading print books came into question with the advent of the digital age. With the mainstream integration of the personal computer in the early 1990s, a paperless society was predicted, and with it the demise of books and traditional libraries. A generation later, it is clear that the prediction was wrong. A much greater quantity of information is available to people today. Much of that information is online, exactly where it should be. However, print, books and libraries are also thriving elements of modern culture. Digital and print formats are associated with different practices of reading. Online reading tends toward rapid scanning, useful for searching and reading snippets. Print is still the superior technology for slow reading anything of length, substance or richness. The prediction of a paperless society should be replaced with that of information ecology, incorporating a spectrum of print and digital technologies.

In "The Slow Movement and Slow Reading", it is observed how the Slow Movement has risen as a response to

the rush of modern life. The movement began with Slow
Food as a protest against fast food. The organization encourages a view that is hard to deny, that slowing down to
prepare and enjoy food increases pleasure in life. A similar
attitude can be taken to reading. Slow Food also emphasizes
the benefits of eating local foods toward agricultural diver-
sity and sustainable farming. A similar theme of locality can
be applied to information. Slow reading can be viewed as
reading local stories and stories by local writers. Libraries
can play an important role as providers of local information
and as micropublishers of local stories. The theme of locality
also plays out around the issue of physical location. Digital
information may seem ethereal, not requiring a library to
house it, but online bookstores struggle to emulate physical
shelves and browsing. E-books are purportedly greener than
print because they do not consume trees, but we are beginning to assess the impact of the Internet on the environment.

The fourth essay, "The Psychology of Slow Reading",
surveys psychological phenomena associated with slow reading. It contrasts the depiction of slow reading as a deficit
against research showing it as a deliberate cognitive strategy. Readers may experience an altered state of consciousness in which the reader becomes "lost" to the book and the
act of reading feels effortless. Bibliotherapy is an unspoken
therapeutic function of a librarian, helping people to cope
through reading. The definition of slow reading is extended
to include any type of reading that deeply engages the
reader's subjective faculties. While it is possible that brains
will someday evolve to read faster, it is also possible that our
brains have evolved to incorporate slowness to make the
most of reading.

Having explored the multifaceted subject of slow reading from these four perspectives, the book concludes with a chapter of suggestions about the practice of slow reading. It is hoped that the book provides a first, full sketch of the breadth of the subject of slow reading, encouraging further research in the area, and inspiring readers to take up slow reading for pleasure.

Chapter 1
The Personal Nature of Slow Reading

Everyone, it seems, wants us to read a message. Our attention is yanked from one bit of information to the next. It hardly feels like reading. We claim to multi-task but in truth we can only give decent attention to one thing at a time. We shift back and forth rapidly, marshalling our cognitive resources on one stimulus only to release it for the next. At best this strategy is inefficient. When it comes to reading anything of length or substance, we miss the meaning entirely. If only we could read faster, we think, perhaps we could manage it all.

A central theme in this book is that reading slowly is often a better choice for comprehension and pleasure in reading. In the past, reading was practiced only by the rare literate person, often in a clerical capacity reading a sacred book with reverence. Later, in the humanities, academics practiced close reading to extract the full meaning of a text. In the modern classroom, educators use slow reading techniques with students of all ages to increase literacy and pleasure in reading. The more successful methods recognize the role of voluntarism in reading. Slow reading is not about reading as slow as possible at all times, but rather exercising the right to slow down at will. The voluntary aspect of slow reading allows for a deep and personal relationship between readers and their information.

Slow Reading in Religion and the Humanities

Modern life has us reading from morning till night -- an ad on a cereal box, headlines and weather on the web, billboards along the road, email and instant messages at work, a credit card statement in the mail. Levy (2001) contrasts this style of reading with the more contemplative style of deep reading associated with books. That deep reading has sacred and reverential qualities is no surprise, for books have their roots in the codex, first adopted by early Christian communities as a vehicle for the Bible. Levy wonders if we experience resonances of the ancestral sacred uses of books. He advises that even in business culture, it is important to develop the capacity for sustained attention rather than just successive attention. By making choices about the stimuli to which we attend, we can draw greater meaning from our experience.

The books of the Bible describe acts of slow reading in the form of bibliophagy, the symbolic eating of a book to gain deep comprehension of a spiritual idea (Peterson, 2006). In the Old Testament, the prophets Ezekiel and Jeremiah ate books by divine command, a preparation for their role as prophets. In the New Testament, an angel told St. John to eat a book, which then was metabolized into his *Book of Revelations*. Eating a book symbolizes a deep and personal internalization of an idea, an intimate act with transformative power. Unlike our modern consumption of information, slow reading is a journey that fundamentally changes us.

Sire (1978) connects slow reading with religiosity in his book, *How to Read Slowly: A Christian Guide to Reading with the Mind*. At first, I found the subtitle an odd one. Why are Christians the intended audience? Sire acknowledges that the practical content can benefit anyone. For example, he advises readers to take the time to read a book's preface and introduction, have a dictionary handy, and read with a pen in hand for notes. Good advice. But Sire's deeper motives are religious. He wants to teach readers to detect the world-view of a writer to see if it squares with Christianity. The reader is advised to apply philosophical questions, e.g., what morality is presupposed? When analyzing fiction, the reader can examine how the plot, theme and characters add up to the author's vision of life. The reader can supplement his or her understanding with biographical, historical, or other contextual information. Sire wisely advises the reader to bring a clear self-understanding to the reading. The subtitle is not so strange after all, since religion deals with deep questions, and Sire's approach is a positive alternative to extremists who would censor books that do not fit their worldview. Still, the techniques are useful to thinkers of any faith.

The eating of books is a recurring metaphor in discussions of slow reading. Bacon used it in his familiar quote about reading:

> Some books are to be tasted, others to be swallowed, and some few to be chewed and digested: that is, some books are to be read only in parts, others to be read, but not curiously, and some few to be read wholly, and with diligence and attention (2001).

Nell observes that as reading rate drops, readers tend to subvocalize, a motor activity of the tongue that mimics eating. "As with a morsel, so with a phrase: rolling it on the tongue for longer than mastication requires extracts its full flavour and nutritive value" (1988, 99).

The earliest explicit reference to the phrase "slow reading" appears to be in Nietzsche's preface to *Daybreak*: "It is not for nothing that one has been a philologist, perhaps one is a philologist still, that it to say, a teacher of slow reading" (1997, 5). Nietzsche views philology as a "connoisseurship of the word" (5) requiring the reader to take the time to read well.

The practice of slow reading continues today in philosophy and the humanities. Quite often, religious scholars will refer to existential philosophers, especially Heidegger. Pike (2004) notes Heidegger's view that "the literary work of art requires that we bring all of ourselves, our spiritual and moral faculties included, to the reading event" (161) and recommended it for studying biblical passages. Others distinguish between religious and philosophical approaches to reading. Smith (2004) argued that a type of slow reading he called aesthetic reading was in fact limited in what it could offer a person's spiritual growth.

Modern reading practices stand in marked contrast to the past when reading was a skill practiced reverentially by the few. If eating a book symbolizes the slow reading of the past, a reverse metaphor is a better fit for today. The exponential growth of information today envelops us, demanding our full attention, almost against our will. It sometimes seems as if the information will eat us up.

The New Criticism and Close Reading

I was not a student of the humanities in university and did not discover at that time the type of slow reading called close reading in literary criticism. Close reading has its origins in the New Criticism, the view that one should pay close attention to the text and language on its own merits, rather than appealing to historical, biographical and cultural sources for interpretation. English students in particular are taught how to analyze a single passage in great depth to extract its layers of meaning.

There may be a reason that I did not hear about close reading outside the halls of the humanities. Debates on the subject of close reading can become quite esoteric. The professional critics distinguish variants in the New Criticism between American and British cultures (Murray, 1991). Other schools of literary criticism object that close reading eclipses political ideas that run deeper than the writer's intentions. The New Criticism is also contrasted with Reader Response Criticism, approaches that focus on the reader's subjective responses rather than the text itself (e.g., Mial & Kuken, 2002). Those of us on the outside may be less interested in these debates.

Academics sometimes treat close reading as a professional practice with highly prescribed techniques. Elder and Paul (2004) defined four structured levels of close reading, with the aim of working one's way into the mind of the author. Students are taught to paraphrase and analyze the text using specific questions and exercises. Learning this approach would take extended instruction and practice.

Stereotypes suggest that literary readers are an elite group, applying techniques hardly amenable to pleasure reading. As such, close reading becomes a professional practice, not a voluntary act. All of this is sufficient to ward off a reader curious about close reading for recreation. It should not be so. Academics often artificially protect their discipline with abstraction. Oz (1999) complains that the literati are doing what her sex education nurse did in her seventh grade – forget to tell the students that the practice is quite fun.

"Only the pleasure of reading do they castrate -- just a bit -- so it doesn't get in the way; so that we remember that literature is not playing games, and, in general, that life is no picnic" (14).

In *Reading Like a Writer* (2006), Prose tells how she used close reading to teach students how to write. She was concerned that many students found reading stressful. In her view, close reading provides a way around this stress. We all begin as close readers, she says, learning to read by listening word-by-word, phrase-by-phrase, to those reading to us. Her view is consistent with Carver's (1990) "rauding" research that matches the process of reading for comprehension to that of listening to speech. In Prose's view, close reading is completely natural.

Prose's book begins with analyzing single words, "Calling her 'the grandmother' at once reduces her to her role in the family" (17). She moves on to sentences -- "can a word or phase be cut from this without sacrificing anything essential?" (43) – and then to paragraphs, and characters, and so on. The essence of the technique is simply to slow down and ask questions.

For Prose, close reading is pleasurable; that is why it works a teaching technique. She tells of the plain fun she had tracing patterns and making connections in her reading at even a young age. Prose's book has been received enthusiastically. Crediting Prose, Grimes (2006) states that the drudgery of reading as information processing only returns to "the sheer bliss of the childhood reading experience … when time, mercifully, stands still." The practice can be called close reading or slow reading or deep reading; it does not matter. Any variant of slow reading can be used to increase comprehension and pleasure in reading.

Slow Reading with Youths

Slow reading has a heritage from religion and the humanities, and with that comes a perception that it is a practice only for advanced readers. That perception is being challenged by teachers who are innovating with slow reading techniques to teach literacy and lasting pleasure in reading to students of all ages.

Metzger (1998) was concerned that her high-school students were not learning how to comprehend difficult text. After researching and experimenting with a number of techniques, Metzger found what she was looking for. She modified a pedagogy known as the Socratic Seminar, a focused discussion on the possible interpretations of a short piece of writing. Her modification entailed an outer circle of students that observes how an inner circle comprehends the text. "In other words, students focus on how they are reading as well as what they are reading." She admits that while the technique cannot make all students love reading, it does give them the skills to comprehend difficult text.

In an earlier version of Metzger's technique, she led the discussion in the inner circle. She agrees with student feedback that it works better when students lead the discussion. Duke (1982) focuses explicitly on this theme, urging teachers to "encourage students to discover the meaning of a text for themselves, using the language of the text and without unnecessary intervention of the teacher." Examples include journal entries and oral reading. This view suggests that slow reading should be voluntary for the best quality of reading experience. Applying a highly prescribed technique or forcing the reading in some way is contrary to the essence of slow reading; to some extent, it must be voluntary for it to be slow reading.

Rereading is a common technique used in close reading. Galef (1998) investigated rereading of narrative texts, including children's literature. He examined how perspectives change after the first reading, and the distortions that emerge through repetition. In examining the gains and losses that go with rereading, he observed that "Rereading has many joys but suspense is not one of them. Anticipation has replaced it." Faust & Glenzer (2000) also used rereading in the classroom. The title of their article came from the testimony of their children: *I could read those parts over and over.* The students readily grasped that rereading literature is like watching movies and listening to music more than once.

Another innovative approach is performance reading. Instead of having students read at their desks or having teachers read Hamlet's soliloquy, Lindblom (2005) used performance methods in English classes. "Performance happens when students look closely at a piece of text and use their voices and bodies to explore the subtleties of the author's words" (116). Lindblom called it "close reading on your feet" and the students loved it. Performance reading requires the performer to process the script in a deeper way, such as imagining how the character feels.

The success of slow reading in the classroom compels an expansion of its meaning. It turns out that slow reading is useful and entertaining for people of all ages. Innovations such as performance reading extend the notion of slow reading to anything that deepens a reader's processing of a text.

The Voluntary Nature of Slow Reading

Prophets might obey divine commands to consume books, and professors might need prescribed techniques for close reading, but the evidence from children is that a voluntary approach is the essence of slow reading.

Taking a look at modern literacy, Krashen (2004) argues that few people are completely unable to read and write. Rather, the modern crisis has to do with the steadily rising demands for literacy. People can read and write, just not well enough. The solution he recommends is free voluntary reading (FVR):

> FVR means reading because you want to. No book report, no questions at the end of the chapter, and no looking up every vocabulary word. FVR reading means putting down a book you don't like and choosing another one instead. It is the kind of reading highly literate people do all the time. (x)

His approach contrasts with direct instruction involving skill building and error correction, and his research shows that FVR yields better comprehension and writing skills. Krashen does not talk specifically about slow reading, but his focus on the voluntary aspect of reading is central to the idea. Let people read the way they want to read, and people will become better readers.

The role of voluntarism is clear when slow reading is contrasted with speed reading. Speed reading refers to methods that increase the rate of reading, such as eliminating the tendency to sub-vocalize when reading. It is associated with the techniques developed by Evelyn Wood (e.g., Frank, 1992). The point of speed reading is to read as fast as possible but slow reading is not the reverse. Slow reading is not about reading as slow as possible. One person savours each word while another skims, slowing down only for certain passages. A book may be read quickly, and then reread years later to gain new insight from maturity. Slow reading may involve arguing with the text, so to speak, or seeking out additional materials to add context. Variability and personal control are essential to slow reading. Slow reading means exercising choice about how one reads rather than being forced to read as fast as possible. This freedom brings back the pleasure of reading.

The Personal Nature of Slow Reading

In the example of performance reading in the classroom, the definition of slow reading was extended to include anything that deepens a reader's relationship with a text, anything that brings more of one's faculties to bear when reading. By this definition, slow reading includes the advanced reader who takes on a difficult work. It includes the reader of a local story that causes a cascade of memories. It also includes the novice reader, struggling mightily with a primer. It should be clear by now that slow reading is open to any reader.

The benefits of slow reading can come from an unpredictable range of reading materials. Prose kept returning to certain writers: Joyce, Tolstoy, Nabokov, and so on, but one does not have to read artistic works to have a deep experience of reading. In his research on ludic reading, Nell (1988) was surprised to find that nearly half of his ludic readers, who describe themselves as reading addicts, rate half their pleasure reading as "trash". Nell challenges "'the elitist fallacy' – the belief that as sophistication grows, coarser tastes wither way" (4). He rejects the distinction between low-brow and high-brow readers, and I agree with him. While I do think that it can be fairly stated that some books are of better quality than others, one cannot say what story or idea will trigger the deep psychological processes associated with slow reading.

The uncertainty around which book will satisfy a reader presents a conundrum for librarians working in a Reader's Advisory capacity. The librarian is confronted with an overwhelming volume of reading material available today. Sutherland (2006) observes that every week more novels are published than Samuel Johnson had to deal with in a decade. He considers the mind-boggling availability of books should everything go online, and the dilemma of how to choose between the good and bad ones. While the availability of books increases the likelihood that a book exists to satisfy the slow reader's particular need, it decreases the probability of finding it. Reminiscent of Socrates, Sutherland advises the reader to "know thy taste", steering him or her away from the marketing ploys of publishers in titles, and provides other sensible advice that should have some use to librarians and readers. Ultimately, however, he agrees with Virginia Wolf who says that no one can give another advice on reading. It is an uncertainty principle of library science.

Chapter 2
Slow Reading in an Information Ecology

Isaac Asimov (1969) tells a story of a future in which a character is asked to demonstrate his astonishing talent to the president. The talent is to perform basic mathematical calculations on paper without the aid of a computer. "'Well', said the president, considering, 'it's an interesting parlor game, but what is the use of it?'"[1] Many writers of fiction and non-fiction express fear that digital technology will render humans less intelligent. Calculations still get performed, but only by computers. People still access information, but through an implant that delivers it instantly. This kind of access to information is the dream of some information providers today, but it is not what we think of as literacy, and certainly not slow reading.

In the 1990s, society witnessed the mainstream integration of personal computers and the web. For a time, it seemed likely that print, books and libraries would disappear, and perhaps literacy along with them. A generation later, we have some evidence by which to assess the reality. The analysis that follows shows that there is a close relationship between the media we use to read – books or digital technology – and the way we read and think. This is not to say that reading on screens spells the end of reading. Digital technology is often preferable for searching and scanning

---

[1] A congressman suggests that replacing expensive computers with humans would allow more investment in peacetime pursuits, but a general imagines the possibility of a lighter, more intelligent "manned missile" that will give them an edge in their war.

short snippets. However, print has endured because it is still the superior technology for reading anything of length, quality or substance. While digital technology lends itself to discovering and remixing ideas in novel ways, slow reading of books is still essential for nurturing literacy and the capacity for extended linear thought.

The Darkest Hour of the Book

The notion of a "paperless office" was coined by Palo Alto Research Center, formerly Xerox, a company known as "the paper people". In a 1970s article in Business Week, George Pake predicted the widespread use of on-screen documents that would largely replace print (Sellen and Harper, 2001). Along with the demise of print is always the prediction of the disappearance of its concomitant entities, books and bricks and mortar libraries. Harris, Hannah & Harris (1998) documented how in 1978, the National Science Foundation awarded a grant to the Library Research Center at the University of Illinois Graduate School of Library Science. The grant funded a report by Frederick Lancaster on the effect of the paperless society on librarianship in 2001. Lancaster rose to prominence as a librarian who promoted a vision of a paperless library. He viewed the book-as-artifact as a major constraint on libraries. What is important to observe is that at the time, Lancaster's vision was a totalizing one. He did not forsee a combination of books and virtual libraries, but a complete displacement of the traditional media in favour of digital technology.

The personal computer was first introduced in the 1980s. It is easy to be nostalgic about those days. It was a significant period for those who were teenagers like myself. It was time when "Generation X" was defined, with a footing in the old world where card catalogues were still the norm in libraries, and a readiness for a new world in which the label of "geek" was about to become cool. I had just enough money from a part-time job to buy one of the inexpensive computers that were being introduced like toys on the market, a Timex Sinclair ZX81. It had black casing, a membrane keyboard, and a whole 2 KB of memory! I used a television for a monitor and an audio tape recorder to save programs. In the days before the web and disk space, it was typical to learn programming from a print computer manual, and type in programs listed in magazines.

For a while, programming displaced my previous entertainment of reading. I had been a regular reader of many kinds of books, including those for the other geek staple, the role-playing game called Dungeons and Dragons. The game involves rolling multi-sided dice to resolve probabilities and the consultation of statistical tables. It was not long till we realized the potential of programming to facilitate the games. We programmed more. We gamed more. The more involved we became, the more books we read too. Writing programs encouraged some of us to try our hand at writing stories. It was a wild and wonderful mix of digital and print technologies.

Things were changing fast. By the end of the eighties, the typewriter, the indispensable tool of writers for over a century, had been superseded by the word processor. In the 1990s, the first e-book readers were introduced in the market. A few years later the web went mainstream. It was no longer enough to have Word on your resume; now you also had to know Netscape or Internet Explorer. Text was going digital. It seemed only a matter of time before the fruition of the vision of a paperless society. One cold night in the mid-nineties we thought we heard a bell toll for print. We waxed nostalgic. It was the price of progress, we said with a sigh. Some inventive folks joked about ways to introduce the smell of books into e-readers, perhaps through scratch 'n sniff cards. Nevermind that print and digital technologies comingled everywhere. In the minds of policy and budget makers, the book was no longer a factor in their plans for the future. In today's language, the book was a legacy technology to be phased out. It was the darkest hour of the book.

We Were Wrong: Print, Books and Libraries are Thriving

The evidence of more than a generation is in: the prediction of a paperless society was in error. Certainly much of what used to be in print is now in digital form. It makes perfect sense that newspapers are dwindling year by year. Despite the crisp feel and smell of a fresh paper, those who want the newest information can find it sooner it on the web. To be sure, stories about the end of print are still trotted out every now and then. A new college claims to be cutting edge because its library is completely digital. One has to wonder if stories like these are not simply spin on a funding shortfall. From the prints on our walls to books on our shelves to the discarded sheets in our recycle boxes, it is clear that print still pervades our lives.

Global consumption of paper products has tripled since the prediction of the paperless office, and is projected to grow by another half before 2010 (World Resources Institute, 1998). That figure includes all paper products but statistics on office paper alone has increased steadily for twenty years (Pulp & Paper International, 2000, July). The illusion of a paperless office is difficult to maintain when we remember that every computer is connected to a printer.

Book sales continue to rise. The Association of American Publishers (2008) indicated a 3.2 percent increase in United States book sales in 2007 over the previous year. Sales of adult and juvenile books grew three percent, with the strongest growth in this category coming from adult hardback books. Audio and e-book sales were up too. People do not want digital books *instead* of print books; they want them both. The overall book pie has grown.[2]

Libraries are also thriving. In 1991, I graduated from university and reflected upon my next step. I considered going to library school but decided against it because I subscribed to the growing perception that print, books and libraries were on the way out. Was I wrong! The nineties were a difficult decade for libraries. In London, Ontario, where I lived, funding for libraries was cut drastically as the municipality struggled to cope with new costs downloaded from the province. I heard about libraries reducing their hours and laying off librarians. It all seemed to fit the pattern. I was not a witness to what happened behind the closed doors of library offices, but it must have been something remarkable. Leaders in the library field must have dug in. Somehow, a new and exciting plan for the London libraries took hold. In time, a new central library was built. Eventually all of the branches enjoyed major renovations. Fifteen years later, I found myself in library school, trying to figure it all out.

There is no doubt that digital technology was a major driver in these changes. The libraries have become popular

---

[2] In December of 2008 there was a lot of talk in book circles about the decline of print publishing, but this decline was true for multiple sectors of the economy due to the global economic crisis.

digital information hubs. The computers likely persuaded funders that libraries still played a relevant role, but there is good evidence that it is the books that kept people coming back. A major environmental scan by the Online Computer Library Center shows that people still overwhelmingly identify libraries with books, print books, as in binding and paper (De Rosa et al, 2005). The massive restructurings to offer digital services go largely unnoticed by users. This finding may dismay those with a futuristic bent, but it should send a signal to the library administrators and budget makers – print books are a secure brand for future planning. Technology should continue to play an increasing role in libraries, but those who exclude books from their plans will get left behind.

Two Explanations for the Persistence of Print

Not everyone believed that print would vanish. If you talked to those who knew books – publishers, librarians, and teachers, especially the older ones – you might find a more sceptical view; but many of us bought into the vision of a paperless society. The fact that so many of us were wrong calls for an explanation. Why does print persist? Why do we still read books the old-fashioned way? There are two possible explanations. One explanation points to the practical problems that have slowed the transition from print to digital technology. A contrasting explanation is that there is something enduring about print that we did not fully appreciate before. It is this second explanation that makes the connection between print and slow reading.

According to the first explanation, it is still only a matter of time before we achieve the paperless society. In his recent book, *Print is Dead,* Gomez (2008) identifies several problems that caused the e-book to fail: high pricing, licensing issues, confusion from the multiplicity of models being offered on the market, and so on. See more such problems in the discussion on e-books later in this chapter. The list is lengthy, but Gomez predicts the problems will get sorted out. Readers will get used to the e-book. Books will become a collector's item, or made like candles by craftspeople. It is interesting to note that many similar problems existed with word processors, such as the confusion caused by competing models, but people did not keep using typewriters.

The availability of digital content is another practical problem. Organizations such as Google and the Open Content Alliance are busy scanning the world's books. The scanning process is both labour-intensive and error-prone. Schillingsburg (2006) observes that 99% accuracy in scanning means an error in every 100 letters, spaces and punctuation marks. "Would we be fatally injured if the word was 'celebrate' not 'celibate' or if the word 'not' is occasionally left out?" (21) Yes, I think. A single typo on a resume will cost an applicant a chance at a job interview.

It is not difficult to continue listing practical problems. Intellectual property rights are easier to protect in a print culture. The associated legal issues need time to get sorted out. Also, some among older generations seem unable or unwilling to adapt to digital technology, but surely the next generation, the digital natives, will be at ease with it. The list is long. What is common to the problems is that they are practical in nature, and can in principle get resolved with time and resourcefulness. I have little doubt that progress will be made. An increasing percentage of information we now read in print will no doubt become digital. What seems less likely is that practical problems explain the whole situation.

The second explanation states that there is something enduring about print that we are just beginning to appreciate,
and will keep it as part of information landscape for the
foreseeable future. If this is so, there must be a hard centre
to print that cannot finally be tackled by future technologi-
cal innovation. It must also be a subtle factor, for many of us
missed it in our rush to the paperless society. The analysis
that follows shows that the hard centre of print is our need
for slow reading. Like many people, I value digital search
for finding quick answers and leads. Reading short snippets
on the web is convenient, and I consider it is wasteful to
print them. However, if the content I have found is anything
longer than a few pages, or if it has any depth, I prefer to
read it in print. Our casual information needs are served
very well by the web, but our reading requirements run
deeper than that. Sometimes we must slow down and read
at a reflective pace and print facilitates that. Print and slowness have a close relationship. Print is fixed; the ideas will
not change during a reading. A book is linear and long, encouraging the reader to recreate the author's original se-
quence of thought. Print persists because it is a superior
technology for integrating information of any length, complexity or richness; it is better suited to slow reading.

Slow Reading Print vs Scanning Online

Books and reading are always understood together. Just
as it was predicted that books would disappear, it was feared
that the habit of reading would dwindle. A number of studies have examined trends in literary reading, the reading of
materials with artistic merit, the kind that might be called
slow reading. In 2004, the National Endowment for the Arts
(NEA) released a report, *Reading at Risk*, a study that investi-

gated literary reading trends in the United States. The study measured literary reading by asking Americans if "during the previous twelve months, they had read any novels, short stories, plays, or poetry in their leisure time (not for work or school)" (ix). It found that "literary reading in America is not only declining rapidly among all groups, but the rate of decline has accelerated, especially among the young" (vii). A follow-up report in 2007, *To Read or Not To Read,* showed a similar pattern for reading in general.

A similar pattern of declining literary reading is described in *The Nation's Report Card 2003* (Donahue, Daane & Jin, 2005). In this case, literary reading is defined as that which "involves the reader in exploring themes, events, characters, settings, plots, actions, and the language of literary works" (4). Material types included novels, short stories, poems, plays, legends, biographies, myths, and folktales. The report explicitly distinguished literary reading from reading for information or to perform a task.

Critics of these studies, e.g., Kirschenbaum (2007), complain that the definition of reading is simplistic, failing to measure other widespread forms of reading taking place on computers and the Internet. Bauerlein, overseer of the 2004 report, responded with other studies showing that only eleven percent of young people go online for information; it is usually for entertainment (Williams, 2005). Bauerlein refers to a well-known study by Nielsen (1997) entitled, *How Users Read on the Web.* The first sentence in the report is, "They don't." Seventy-nine percent of their test users always scanned the page, picking out words and sentences rather than reading word by word. Eye-tracking studies by Weinreich et al (2008) found that on average, web users read at most twenty-eight percent of the words on a page. Nielsen's advice to editors is "to cut 40 percent of the word

count while removing only 30 percent of an article's value"
(2007). This approach is unquestionably efficient. It would
also brutalize any literary writing a slow reader might hope
to find online.

The proponents of the paperless society assumed that
people would simply transfer their reading to the screen. It
is interesting to note that early studies about reading the
web showed people still reading faster with print, though the
explanation was not easy to pin down (Dillon, 1992). There
were limitations such as image quality at the time, but part
of the reason may be that people were still trying to adapt
their print reading skills to the web. Reading online is quite
different from reading print. For example, it is the essence
of hypertext to point the reader away from the page being
read. Print does not have this distraction and so is better
suited to slow reading. If digital technology served all styles
of reading, then print should have vanished by now. Some
literary readers may have tried to read online and found it
unsatisfactory. Those who are still literary readers, slow
readers, are doing it in print. Some may have switched their
reading habits to scan the web. It follows that if more people
are reading online, then less slow reading is occurring.

Slow Reading is Deeper than Technology

A persistent fear about technology is that it undermines
literacy and the capacity for critical thinking. Postman
(1986) laments the decline of the Age of Typography which
had its zenith in the 19th century. He notes the character of
mind of the ordinary citizen of the day, who could listen for
hours on end to political orations clearly shaped by a culture
favouring text. Speeches would be followed by equally literate and equally lengthy rebuttals. The citizens who took

time for this process were the same ones working dawn to dusk farming the lands. These people were well equipped to shape their nation. The Age of Television, on the other hand, is characterized by entertainment designed to please the eye. It requires no literacy and no reflective mental processing. We evaluate ourselves through the eye of television, and judge our politicians through their showmanship. As Postman warns, reading books is important for developing rational thinking, character of mind and political astuteness. From this view, what is good in modern politics is sustained by the citizenry with the patience for serious reading.

Birkerts (1994) denounces digital media for the decline of literacy. Referring to literature, he says "the overall situation is bleak and getting bleaker .... Book buying and reading have fallen off radically among the under-thirty crowd. And who can guess what the numbers will look like as new generations come of age?" (190). He is certain that our electronic culture is injuring our capacity to read: "We may have altered our cognitive apparatus – speeding up, learning to deal with complex assaults of stimuli – in such a way we can no longer take in the word as it is meant to be taken in" (191). Birkerts recommends "deep reading: the slow and meditative possession of a book" (146).

Baron (2005) acknowledges that the rise of computer-based communications has led to an increase in the production and sales of print materials; but she is concerned that it may conceal changes to traditional written culture. She identifies a number of watch points to monitor, including the existence of serious readers, hand-writers and traditional forms of writing like diaries rather than blogs. She calls to observation the dissolution of the individual author, the replacement of copyright by licensing, the replacement of publishing by on-demand printing by individuals, and a decline in language standards.

In his recent article, *Is Google Making Us Stupid?*, Carr (2008) describes his uncomfortable feeling that the Internet is remapping his neural circuitry. He can feel it most strongly when he's reading. He finds it increasingly difficult to read a lengthy article or book. He cites a University College London study which studied visitors' behaviour at research sites. They found that people were skimming, not reading in the traditional sense. He wonders if Google's plans to perfect the search engine will have undesirable consequences on our capacity to think.

There is merit in monitoring these changes, but the fears should be tempered by the fact that they were shared by others who predate digital technology. In 1904, Nicoll wrote *The Lost Art of Reading* to respond to concerns that reading was seen as a vice, bad for work. In 1907, Lee wrote a book of the same title, seeing the lifestyle at the time as too rushed, urging people to slow down and read. Digital technology alone is not a threat to reading, but rather the proclivity to speed up life to the point that reading becomes problematic. Digital technology is typically used to make life more efficient, but to some extent reading will be at odds with efficiency. Reading takes up time, and it has the power to conjure us away from the present moment. It speaks to inner faculties not always easily processed with the frame of our daily routine. It makes us think. Reading and slowness go hand in hand. It has always been a target for those who would have us more productive.

Fears that reading is vanishing must also be reconciled with another frequent claim, that reading is a great pleasure. It seems odd that a pleasurable activity would be on the decline. Perhaps it does not seem so odd if we consider that reading requires an investment of inner resources that people may be less willing to make. Like cooking a good meal or nurturing a relationship, and unlike fast food or too much television, reading is one of those cardinal pleasures that require effort upfront but leaves the reader feeling more energized afterward. This is another reason that reading is at risk in every generation, but especially in the digital age. Our attention can only manage so many stimuli. With the endless stream of information fed to us in modern life, our attention is compromised. The web was supposed to make information more manageable, but in fact it displaces time and attention we might spend really savouring a good read.

Reading is connected to literacy and critical thinking, but digital technology is not the primary villain. The real problems are our weakness for speed and our attempts to attend to too many things at once. We cannot accelerate our lives indefinitely. At some point we have to slow down to get a handle on our information. Slow reading represents balance.

Print is the Next Big Thing

The historical timing of inventions does not always correspond to the brilliance and importance of the same. Print led to digital text, much like the wheel led to the automobile. Sometimes we forget how much of modern life depends on these old technologies. Print enlists the hands in the act of reading, signalling the brain where to read next, and how much more there is to read. Digital reading shifts all the work to the eyes. Sellen and Harper (2001) observe that print is still the best medium for many purposes, including conceptual design, editing, proofreading, sensing the flow of text, and finally as a tangible bound object: "Ultimately, we want a bound volume in hand – a physical product that testifies to our efforts and that we can hand to family, friends, and colleagues" (1).

Print has its own limitations. It takes a heavy toll on the environment. When I am simply trying to catch the headlines or look up a definition, I do not need print, and should only print as a last resort. The print version of TV Guide was recently sold for a dollar. This makes perfect sense since television programming can change by the hour. On the other hand, the length of the average book has grown from 400 to 500 pages between 1995 and 2005 and "wordy" magazines like Atlantic Monthly and Foreign Affairs are increasing in circulation (Penn, 2007). When I wish to understand something, I often begin a search with Google. This is only problematic if searches always end there. The most perfect home for information snippets is online; they can be easily indexed, searched and scanned. When the snippets are inadequate, scrolling is substandard, hyperlinks are leading nowhere, and notifications are distracting me, that is, when slow reading is required, then print is the superior choice for reading.

E-Book Readers Aspire to Print

The web has subsumed a fair quantity of short information media -- flyers, brochures, television listings, news and so forth. Too much advertising still shows up on my front porch, but there has been a relatively successful shift of this kind of content to the web. Many people find it more desirable to read this kind of information on our computer screens. Longer, book-sized content can also be found on the web in a variety of e-book formats, including the common portable document format (PDF) that can be viewed in most web browsers. E-books are a compelling idea – they replace the size and weight of physical books with a small file, and integrate full-text searching. Still, most find the format a degraded reading experience. I have seen people flip their laptops 90 degrees to simulate a print book, but it still does not work for in-depth reading. There is a trend in Japan to read books by cell phone. Each day, a short piece of a book is texted to the subscriber. Shortness of length seems to be the success factor for readability of information using digital technology, at least for multi-purpose devices such as personal computers and cell phones.

A sensible response to this shortcoming is a dedicated, digital reading device, designed expressly for enhanced readability. Every couple of years a new e-book reader is announced on the market, most recently the Amazon Kindle and the Sony Reader. The essential design element in these devices is "bookishness". Bezos, CEO of Amazon.com, says of the Kindle, "it should be less of a whizzy gizmo than an austere vessel of culture" (2007, November 26). Everything about the Kindle is designed to make it more like a book. It has the dimensions of a paperback and is tapered to emulate the bulge of a book's binding. Earlier models of e-books had a back-lit display like a monitor that can cause eye strain. The Kindle and the Reader use e-ink, a technology designed to simulate real print. Battery life has been extended so that the device will not shut down during a length read in the park.

Bezos intends nothing less than the replacement of the print book, "Books are the last bastion of the analog." While the vendors have enjoyed a certain success in sales, they have not succeeded in replacing the book. As with the failed prediction about the paperless society, one can explain the persistence of the print book using two kinds of explanations. The first kind of explanation has to do with practical problems that can be resolved in time. Look at the price of the readers: $400 USD for the Kindle and $300 CAD for the Sony Reader is steep when I can still borrow my books from the library for free. Kindle licensing prohibits lending of its readers at libraries (Oder, 2008, February 7). The vendors are entitled to profit from their products, but this leads to irritating conditions like being locked into buying titles from the vendor alone. These problems could be resolved in time as mass production lowers prices and Kindle modifies its licensing. Other transient problems have to do with design flaws. One cannot flip pages like a book or compare two documents side-by-side. Inventive people are working hard to engineer solutions to these problems. Researchers at Maryland and Berkeley Universities have developed a prototype dual-display e-book reader (Chen et al, 2008). It has two screen faces, connected in the middle like binding. When the reader fans one of the faces, the page turns, much like a book. I look forward to being able to use devices like this.

A closer look at the trend in e-book reader engineering points to the second kind of explanation about why the print book persists. When digital technology first went mainstream people began to imagine how the book would change. In most cases, efforts were made to make the book more like the computer, hence e-books in PDF format. What has changed for the better since then is that engineering efforts are dedicated to make computers more like books. It is the express goal of the vendors to make their e-book readers like print books. The pursuit of this goal may ultimately be self-defeating. While print books have many features that resist digitalization, it has one fundamental feature that undercuts the need for digital technology: fixity.

Print has the virtue of capturing an idea in a fixed form so that it can be read slowly and processed. Brain function is always a combination of neural excitation and inhibition. An inability to inhibit neural activity is associated with disorders such as epilepsy. Neural inhibition requires fixity, giving the brain the opportunity to open deeply to a text, to evaluate it without concern that it will change. You cannot click away. There are no message notifications. For slow reading, I seldom need full-text searching because I am trying to recreate the author's original intentions, reading in the linear format the ideas as they were intended to be read. E-book readers can only mimic this state by turning off all the bells and whistles. At that point, what does the reader really provide beyond the print book? For the e-book to serve the purposes of slow reading, it must become a print book.

Most readers wisely take a pragmatic position. E-book readers meet certain needs better than print books. The readers can hold multiple books, perform full-text searching, increase print-size for the visually impaired, and download and process payments for new books at the press of a button. As long as they still prefer print books for some kinds of reading, then the two forms of books will continue to co-exist. It is a sensible attitude. It is a different matter altogether for the designers and sellers of digital reader technology. Despite all their efforts, for some kinds of reading – long-form reading, slow reading -- the print book is the superior technology. Obvious to many who read, this insight is a tragedy to those hoping to make a fortune by improving upon the book.

E-Books are Metadata for Print Books

In the early days of digital technology it was trendy to talk
about artificial intelligence, especially if you were an entre-
preneur trying to sell software. It was a popular conception
that digital technology could think for us. No doubt by the
turn of the millennium we would be having conversations
with computers, hopefully issuing orders that they would
carry out for us. Things turned out somewhat differently.
The current trend of Web 2.0 attempts to harness the col-
lective intelligence of its users, not the intelligence of the
software. The effectiveness of Google, Wikipedia, Delicious,
and so forth lies in the content generated by its users. Cynics
might see this approach as a clever trick to get people to
work for free. In any case, the reality of digital technology
has trended quite differently than originally imagined.
Technology has limitations that can only be compensated
by traditional sources – people, print, books.

Books are not being replaced by digital technology. Instead of reading online, websites are increasingly offering
online services to enhance the experience of reading print
books. The WorldCat catalogue of the Online Computer
Library Center (OCLC) helps people find books in their
local libraries. Web 2.0 startups like LibraryThing allow
users to catalogue their books online. Literary websites are
using GoogleEarth to show people the literary heritage of
their cities (Irvine, 2008). Many people were surprised to
learn that Wikipedia, the online encyclopedia, was being
printed by a German publisher (Cohen, 2008, April 23).
Digital technology is adapting to the constancy of the book.

Pundits declaring the end of the book admit the irony of
publishing their books in print (Gomez, 2008; Jarvis, 2008).
The usual explanation is that people and publishers have

not made the transition yet. In this view, the coexistence of print and digital realms is a negative thing. Doctorow is a science fiction writer who sees the web quite differently. He distributes free full-length e-books of his works from his website. As he sees it, his readers will be grateful for the freebies, become evangelists of his work and ultimately buy more print books than if he remained in obscurity (2006). The book's first printing sold out months ahead of the publisher's expectations (Lessig, 2004). It is a trend that is catching on (Darbyshire, 2007; Gaiman, 2008). From this perspective, print and digital technologies co-exist as happy complements.

The success of Doctorow's experiment is evidence in favour of the view espoused in this chapter that print and books persist because of enduring qualities. There is no dispute that digital technology brilliantly serves some purposes never available in print culture. Search functions in particular are much easier than the old days of digging through print indexes. It is also true that reading short snippets on the web is quite an acceptable reading experience; it should be encouraged given the environmental cost of wasteful printing. However, to read anything of length or substance, to read slowly, we need print books for their superior readability. All of this points to an emerging model in which digital representations of books can be viewed as metadata for finding print books. The web provides a resource for storing traditional metadata about a book, such as title, author, and so on. Since readers prefer to read print books, even a full-text representation of a book is metadata because it exists only for evaluative purposes before the reader seeks out the physical copy. It is a wonderful arrangement for readers because the increased availability of metadata, along with digital search, means increased ease of finding the best reading materials. The boundary between digital and print worlds is not a soft one to be removed in time, but instead a hard centre enduring around the need for slow reading.

The Big Picture: An Information Ecology

The contrast between print and digital technologies in this chapter has oversimplified the situation a bit. There are a wide variety of print and digital technologies, and there are technologies for information exchange other than print and digital media. A continuum can be drawn with print on the left pole and digital technology on the right. Print-on-demand devices could be said to occupy a middle-ground because it takes advantage of both digital and print technologies. Further to the left I might place "stone tablets" like the ones we are told were used to record the Ten Commandments. Stone tablets are even more fixed than print, and are still a part of our information culture. Further to the right I might place "ideas" in a Platonic sense, more ethereal than digital representations. Instead of just talking about print and digital technology, we see that information technology is a complex domain, distinguished by degrees but still sharing a common dimension. This kind of continuum ties into emerging models of information such as pace layering. Morville (2005) describes pace layering as a house; with Web 2.0 technologies like tagging corresponding to highly changeable surfaces like walls; and traditional library classification corresponding to the enduring concrete foundation.

One could also use a metaphor of leaves and a tree to describe the complexity of the relationships between information technologies. This metaphor comes from nature, suggesting an organic system, an information ecology, including not only the technologies but the people who use it. Nardi and O'Day (1999) state, "In information ecologies, the spotlight is not on technology, but on human activities that are served by technology" (49). Libraries are a clear example of an information ecology, with books, magazines, DVDs, and computer terminals. It also has librarians for whom access to information of all kinds for all people is a core value. Libraries house a complex range of information activities, be that story time for two-year-olds, a poetry recitation by a local author, or a podcasting workshop. It is no wonder that libraries have thrived through the digital age. They are one of the few places that respond to the complexity of our information needs.

Reading too is a complex phenomenon in our information ecology. Ross (2006) points out that literacy is a moving target. "Whereas in the nineteenth century, the measure of literacy was being able to sign one's name instead of an X on a document, expectations are now far higher. To be literate in a modern society means not only being able to read documents but being able to use them effectively in everyday life contexts." (3). She suggests it is a misunderstanding of youth to dismiss online reading as an enemy of reading. She argues for an expanded definition of reading, including everything from the serious scholar to the gamer with a digital help file. I am in strong agreement with this view. The arguments in favour of slow reading are not intended to denigrate the advances of digital technology, but rather to clarify its position in our information ecology.

Chapter 3
The Slow Movement and Slow Reading

After a pressured day in his world of advertising there seemed to be no solution to the problems thrashing around in the head of Sydney Piddington. In *The Special Joys of Super-Slow Reading* (1973), Piddington recounts his decision to relax by spending three hours on two chapters of a book, "I lost myself in the author's world, *living* his book. And when I finally put it down, my mind was totally refreshed." (157). Ironically, this article was published in *Reader's Digest*. On the back flap was an advertisement directed to women for the magazine's condensed books: "To every Miss, Mrs. And Ms. who has no time to read – READ THIS!" Piddington understood what his publishers did not, that slowing down is essential in the rush of modern culture.

Piddington wrote his article in 1973 before the main-stream integration of the personal computer and other digital technologies into our lives. Technology does make life easier in many ways but we tend to accept it unreservedly, forgetting that each solution comes with its own set of problems. As an information technology professional, I appreciate how web access allows me to work from home, but I also find it difficult to mentally let go at the end of the work day. I wind up checking work email when I would rather be playing ping-pong with my son. No doubt every generation has felt rushed, but the accelerating presence of technology in our lives comes with escalating costs. We pay for the constant speed with reduced performance, burnout, impaired relationships, and sometimes even our lives.

Increasing numbers of people are getting fed up with the rush of modern life and are choosing instead to slow down. Honoré (2004) is the author of the book, *In Praise of Slow: How a Worldwide Movement is Changing the Cult of Speed*, which documents the rise of the Slow Movement. In 1986, McDonald's opened another one of their restaurants in Rome. Fed up with fast food, Carlo Petrini protested by starting Slow Food, an organization that promotes the pleasures and payoffs of eating fresh local foods produced in season by sustainable farming practices. Slow Food International currently claims over 85,000 members in 132 countries (2008). Honoré traces the development from Slow Food to other movements. Slow Cities is intended to recreate urban life based on the principles of Petrini. Others practice slow exercise, slow sex, slow work, slow parenting and so on. It's a global reaction against acceleration.

Honoré's interest in the Slow Movement began with slow reading. One day in an airport he spotted a newspaper article on a series of condensed fairy tales called *The One-Minute Bedtime Story*. At first it struck him as brilliant — the cure to his nightly tug-of-war with his son's demands for more stories — then the absurdity of his fast lifestyle called him to his senses. These days (2007), he goes into son's room, leaving his watch behind and his computer speaker turned off so he does not hear the pings of email deliveries, and slows down to his son's pace, talking about whatever as they read a story. It has changed from a task to be hurried to a reward to be cherished.

Speed is not anathema to the Slow Movement. Not everything should be done as slowly as possible. It is only that our obsession with speed has turned into an addiction. Slowing down tends to improve life. At work, a slower pace tends to increase overall performance. Slow reading increases literacy skills. Waters, executive editor for the humanities at Harvard, declared a worldwide reading crisis resulting from our global push toward productivity. Young children are learning to read faster, skipping phonetics and diagramming sentences; these children will not grow up to read Milton. Foreseeing the end of graduate English literature programs, he advised re-introducing time into reading, "People are trying slow eating. Why not slow reading?"(2007). The benefits of slow reading can be academic or more pedestrian. Mid-afternoon at work, I get a lift just thinking about the escapist novel I have waiting for me at home.

Slow Reading and Locality

The Slow Movement began with Slow Food and its protest against fast food and fast life. Their philosophy claims a right to good food. It is easy to see how this philosophy applies to others things in life such as good books. It is not uncommon to find connections made between food and books, and a desire for slow reading follows easily on the heels of slow food. On some level, both food and books are essential elements of the good life.

The most obvious sense of slowness in reference to quality is temporal – we stop racing against the clock to better appreciate a meal or a book. One cannot talk about the temporal sense for long before getting into the second sense as well, that of space. Time and space are hinged together. This need not become a metaphysical discussion; simply put, you slow down in speed and you automatically cover less distance. When you slow down in speed, the world at hand becomes more salient. You get more involved with people and events in your neighbourhood.

The Slow Food movement brings out this less obvious sense of slowness, the spatial one, in its views on locality; that is, geographic proximity. Fast food is manufactured according to standardized recipes, mostly on assembly lines, shipped across the globe to its franchises. The aim is consistency in branding and customer expectations. Mass production of food can result in lower prices, but also low quality bland food, a diminishment of local culinary knowledge, a weakening of regional agricultural infrastructure, and environmental damage. Slow Food seeks to protect local food traditions, biodiversity and farming. Fast food necessitates the idea of a consumer because people are distanced from their food sources and production processes. Slow Food considers people to be "co-producers, not consumers" (2008) because their food is produced locally and they personally support its production.

The theme of locality from Slow Food adds dimension to the meaning of slow reading. Fast books are those produced for the broadest possible appeal, stamped out in assembly lines and distributed at points of maximum exposure such as Amazon or warehouse-sized bookstores. Fast books may be associated with movie deals and celebrity endorsements. This situation is frightfully depicted in Redekop's fictional work, *Shelf Monkey*. Fast reading is also associated with reading on the web, where people tend to scan content rather than read slowly. Slow books, on the other hand, may be characterized by local events which may be of great interest to residents and visitors seeking to learn more about a particular region, but too limited in market appeal for mass production. Slow books are not written so much for profit as for pleasure, developing a local tradition in writing and micro-publishing. As with Slow Food, there is a much closer connection between readers and their information.

The relationship between local foods and local reading comes out in Smith & MacKinnon's (2007) *The 100-Mile Diet: A Year of Local Eating*, a record of their efforts to eat only local foods for a one-year period. They talk about the traceability of their food: "They know exactly where their food comes from, and under what circumstances it was produced" (54-55). Local foods and traditions necessarily come equipped with first-hand knowledge since they are taught by locals to community members. This autochthonous knowledge is missing in our web-based information. Schools may teach students to properly cite their sources but the authorship of web-based materials is often uncertain and these materials can change or vanish. It is not uncommon for people to forget an author's name, let alone know the context in which he or she wrote the book. Slow readers, on the hand, seek out the writers and places associated with local stories.

One can imagine a book entitled, *100-Mile Stories: A Year of Local Reading*. I might find listed the down and dirty, true tale of the Donnelly clan; and how they wronged virtually everyone in the pioneer town of Lucan, Ontario, only a few miles from my home (Kelley, 1994). The grammar is strained, the perspective is biased, and I wouldn't change a thing. After reading this book, I went to visit the Roman Line in nearby Lucan. "The farther down the road you go, the tougher the folks get, and the Donnellys live in the last house." The original house had been burned down and there was little to indicate the Donnellys once lived there, but I swear I heard an echo of "my own grave being dug." This book is not literary reading, but it is slow reading because it engages memories and feelings only a local resident will share.

The local dimension of slow reading also fits with Birkets' (1994) idea of vertical reading. Birkets observes that the ar-

rival of the printing press resulted in the production of far
more books on a wider range of topics. It enabled what he
calls horizontal reading, "a shift from intensive to extensive
reading" (72). Horizontal reading takes us outward, expos-
ing us to new ideas from out in the world. The freshness of
vertical reading does not come so much from exposure to
new material, but from drawing more deeply on our current
experience. Rosenblatt (1994) emphasizes the personal factors a person brings to a reading. Personal history, a current
situation, as well as thoughts and feelings condition the
reader's response. The reading is local in a geographical
sense because a reader comes from some physical place that
defines his or her perspective. The reading is also local in a
psychological sense since it is coloured by the reader's pre-
occupations and cares. The psychological analysis of slow
reading is developed further in the next chapter.

Libraries as Producers of Slow Information

Fast information is often a good thing. I like the conven-
ience of paying bills from home, the ability to download
music or to order goods online. The downside is spam,
automated telemarketers and all the other variants of information overload that seem inevitable in modern life. It is
easy to complain about advertising and automation, but few
of us would complain if we found just the right information
at the right time. The problem is one of relevance and it
goes to the heart of information technology. Activities can
only be automated with software to the extent that they con-
form to general rules. It would defeat the purpose of software to program it for each situation. Localized data provides a solution only to the extent that it has been entered
by someone who knows it. Users of web-based mapping

programs like Google Maps and MapQuest often find the general directions accurate, e.g., freeways, but find the local directions inaccurate or inefficient. Town residents know which streets have recently been changed or are under construction, but this data does not get uploaded. As the old saying goes about food, eat where the locals eat. Local information is a slower kind of information complementing the fast information on the web.

Libraries have long been providers of local data. Lyons (2007) notes that libraries traditionally provide community information on employment opportunities, local businesses, social services, education, recreation, local government and community organizations. But why stop there? Tapping into the "long tail" of Web 2.0, the eclectic niche information not found anywhere else, Lyons recommends that libraries specialize in generating detailed local information and uploading to the web. In this view, libraries are hubs of slow information, producers of local content, and an important complement to the centralized stores of giants like Google who cannot be bothered to collect it.

Library cataloguing is another area that has seen the benefits and costs of information technology. The Online Computer Library Center (OCLC) is a centralized resource to which libraries upload their cataloguing data. OCLC publishes this data to its web-based WorldCat catalogue. An upside of this arrangement is that web users can find the closest library that has a particular item available. The downside is that it excludes libraries with budgets too small to afford membership. Getting bigger is not the solution. Information technology requires standardized cataloguing practices. Standardization skims off the local variations, the most important data for granular analysis of a community. OCLC could offer grants to let small libraries participate but this would not solve the standardization problem. One solution would be to maintain two sets of cataloguing data: one standardized set for efficient high-level searching, and a second localized set for detailed low-level searching. The two sets could be combined in a federated search.

Libraries could also become independent publishers of local stories using both digital and traditional media. Blogs are a popular low-cost digital media. It may be objected that local stories are not necessarily of good quality or of any interest to the world. Since blogs are unedited, they just add to the noise. Extending the slow food metaphor, a local burger is still just fast food. The truth in this objection could be ameliorated by librarians serving an editorial role, but there are also other benefits to be considered. Just as slow food helps develop the local food industry, so too local storytelling and publishing helps develop local authors and the arts community. Also, while the global publishing industry does filter out low quality material, it also filters out a lot of good and divergent voices that do not have sufficient market appeal. Take for example a group of second language students who were discouraged by the lack of materials at an adult level and created about 400 books to be kept for other students (Dupuy & McQuillan, 1997). Print media lends itself to diversification of content. Libraries can tap into the swelling book arts movement. These books represent a special collection, always the hottest item for library visitors and scanning initiatives (Greek, cited in Miller, 2008, August 15). Even the global media will come looking for this content when its audience wearies of the banal content of mass programming.

Information Has a Location

Libraries have long been considered the physical embodiment of knowledge, the home of shelves of books. Within the library, one can be sure to find every item in the collection catalogued with a specific call number. In this ordered world, information clearly has a location. The advent of the web has called this view under scrutiny. People can call up information on a computer from home or on the road. Hyper Text Markup Language (HTML) has been supplemented by Extensible Markup Language (XML) which cleanly separates webpage data from its presentation format. A user can request data in HTML, portable document format (PDF) or other formats, by browser, cell phone or other devices. Instead of the traditional hierarchical classification schemes, social software sites use folksonomy -- user generated tags -- to organize information. Folksonomy is criticized for its lack of controlled vocabulary and for unclear relations between terms, but it requires much less labour than formal classification and users seem satisfied with it. Information seems ethereal, transcending the limits of physical embodiment.

Of course libraries are more than just data, they provide a context to information and a house to the people who use it. Earlier this year, I had the opportunity to tour Salt Lake City's Public Library. I had seen a picture of it on the web but that was nothing like the actual physical library, with its six-story, curving, walkable wall wrapping around 240,000 square feet of building, topped with gardens in view of the city and the Wasatch Mountains. Easily the most delightful space was the children's play areas, including Grand-Mother's Attic with a trunk of dress-up clothes and the fantastic Crystal Cave. Separating the data from format in those cases is a bit more of a challenge.

When it comes to books, one finds innovative website designers struggling to reconnect users with physical context. Amazon, for example, has launched two recent prototypes that try to recreate a real bookstore feel, including Windowshop which lets users browse items with audio and visual enhancements (Amazon, 2008a) and Zoomii which lets users scroll around real looking bookshelves (Amazon, 2008b). Clearly, the physical dimensions of information are still vital.

The science fiction writer, William Gibson, coined the term, "cyberspace", to refer to a separate digital realm that is freed from the constraints of the physical world. Marketers of cutting edge miasma computing play into that term. Miasma computing promises a separation of physical hardware from users. It is possible to change servers in a moment with the notice of users. It is marketed as "cloud computing" as if the servers are out in cyberspace, a tempting prospect for businesses who do not want to worry about hardware. The idea of a separate ethereal cyberspace makes for good storytelling and marketing, but it caters to a false perception. Humans, computers and information have always co-existed in the same physical space. Every bit of data is stored on a physical computer and every exchange of data is a physical event. The Internet is a massive hardware infrastructure, occupying space and consuming resources. Jonathan Schwartz (2005), CEO of Sun Microsystems, observed, "Google's and Yahoo!'s second largest operating expense - after the people they employ is ... electricity. That's why they're building datacenters next to smelting plants." The Internet is a large, hungry creature placing a heavy footprint on our planet.

Slow Reading is Green

Purveyors of e-books and other digital products often claim that their products are better for the environment since they do not consume paper. It is true that print is environmentally expensive. Haggith (2008) describes the environmental damage caused by the print production process and recommends good ways to reduce our dependence on paper. However, technology also takes a toll, just in a different way. Toxic waste from computer hardware and batteries fills dumps. Some full lifecycle assessments have found a marginal environmental benefit of digital over print technology (Moberg et al, 2007; Kozak, 2003) but the research in this area is nascent. It must be recognized that the production of print escalated dramatically with the advent of digital technology. Every computer is connected to a printer. In the earlier days of print culture, better quality materials were created for endurance and reuse. These cultural factors have not been assessed.

In chapter two, a connection was made between slow reading, print and literacy. A connection can also be made between slow reading, print and a cognitive style that may favour the complex analysis required to address environmental problems. Reading on the web tends to be scanning rather than slow reading. Online, there is competition for attention between hyperlinks, ads, instant messages, email messages, and so on. This dynamic environment favours a style of thinking that can be quite useful. It allows remixing of unlike ideas and can lead to innovative solutions. Slow reading creates a different kind of thinker. Slow reading a substantive text to its end, without distraction, allows the reader to recreate in his or her imagination the author's original ideas. The reader is compelled to be sensitive to subtle patterns as they emerge. It creates a capacity for extended linear thought, the ability to follow complex chains of logic. The environment is a complex problem; its complexity makes it easier to ignore. Who is willing to take a hit in their daily standard of living? Better, it seems, to leave the problem to governments and scientists. Linear thinkers can see the subtle patterns emerging from their personal lifestyles, and appreciate the long-term chain of events from their actions today. Slow reading is a vital skill in nurturing this way of thinking.

Chapter 4
The Psychology of Slow Reading

In *The Singularity Is Near: When Humans Transcend Biology*, futurist Ray Kurzweil (2005) envisions a time when accelerating developments in technology will lead to a merger of human intelligence with machines. His vision is a fantastic one. Perhaps advanced brains like this will be able to absorb information both at an incredible pace and with penetrating depth. There is reason to be doubtful. Futurism is an error-prone business, with predictions based on current trends without adjusting for counterbalancing factors. Perhaps one day information will be everywhere, only to be plucked instantly from the ether whenever we need it, and minds will be engineered to absorb much larger quantities of information than is possible today. Will the information mean the same thing? Can it maintain the desirable qualities associated with slowness, such as intimacy and sociability? If not, we must seek them outside of technology. Reading research and studies in psychology and neuroscience suggest that slowness is in fact an important factor in understanding how we read and think.

Controlled Studies of Slow Reading

It is relatively easy to find controlled studies on the problematic aspects associated with involuntary slow reading. It is less easy to find studies on slow reading as a deliberate strategy. There are some. For example, Hyönä & Nurminen (2006) found that adult readers are aware of both their reading speed, lookback and rereading behaviour. Looking back was positively correlated with recall of the text. That is, slow reading behaviours are a deliberate cognitive strategy used to improve the reading experience.

Another type of slow reading research looks at the benefits of reduced reading rates to comprehension. In Carver's (1990) seminal work on rauding theory he proposed five "gears" of reading. Unlike the first two gears of scanning and skimming, the third gear, "rauding", includes comprehension and it is what we normally think of as reading. (He calls it rauding because he views reading and auding – listening to words – as the same process). The last two gears are learning and memorizing; they are slower and even more powerful than rauding. Carver found that most people read at a constant rate, their rauding rate, and it is best for comprehension of relatively easy material. When difficult material is encountered, individuals will temporarily shift down to slower rates of reading.

Carver's research shows that slower modes of reading are required for comprehension of more complex material. I would only add that slow reading involves more than the learning and memorizing behaviours associated with Carver's fourth and fifth gears. The present book has explored other methods such as performance reading and the reading of local stories in developing a deep understanding of information. I prefer Yoakam's four types of reading, with the fourth being called "careful reading, which included assimilative and analytic reading" (cited in Carver, 1990, 13). Careful reading seems a better label for slow reading and its multitude of methods.

Research on the positive value of slow reading is easier to find when the definition is expanded to include any sort of reading that profoundly engages the reader. Reader Response Criticism is a type of literary criticism that focuses on the reader's subjective responses to a text. These responses have been a subject of studies employing experimental techniques and questionnaires. Miall and Kuiken (2002), for example, proposed four levels of feeling during literary reading. At the highest level, aesthethic and narrative feelings produce events in the reader, including identification and catharsis, and modify the reader's self-understanding. These profound responses change the reader. If the reader of the future had to evolve to process these changes more quickly, it would difficult to be sure that these subjective responses would be anything like those experienced by a slower brain.

Slow Reading as a State of Consciousness

Without subscribing to a stereotype, there is something to the image of a reader as a solitary soul, lost in a book. Slow reading has been characterized as an activity that deeply engages the faculties of the reader. Research on avid reading and ludic reading describes a similar phenomenon.

Ross (2006) takes a close look at the subjective experience of readers. She interviews readers and examines autobiographical accounts, such as Schwartz's (1996) *Ruined by Reading: A Life in Books*. When I picked up Schwartz's book, I was reading *A Tale of Two Cities*, the book she claims won out over childhood lessons in the housewifely arts; no surprise there. My copy of Dickens is a lovely old book, picked up as part of a collection at an estate sale. The pages are yellowing, but the smell is entrancing. If I cannot read it for an evening, I will read only a few pages at a time, in between chores like Schwartz. Even those few minutes are important to me, the moments that keep me sane the rest of the day. It is a sort of altered state, and this is consistent with the repeating themes in Ross' research. Avid readers find reading a happy surrender, transporting the reader through language to another place.

Nell's (1988) research on "ludic" or pleasure reading indicates that some readers may experience an altered state of consciousness. Nell discusses how ludic reading is not just absorption associated with laboured attention on a difficult text. Ludic reading is "entrancement, transporting us to other places and transfiguring our consciousness to make other people of us" (199). Many readers describe this kind of reading as effortless. It is effortless, but not necessarily rapid. There is substantial rate variability during natural reading, with most-liked pages being read significantly slower. While it has some similarities to other altered states, ludic reading appears to be a distinct state, e.g., unlike dreams, book fantasy never becomes overwhelming, it is a "safe place" that "allows readers to enjoy a kind of sovereignty over their lives and worlds" (226). The model of sovereignty is a good one for capturing the idea of reading as a world unto itself.

Slow reading might involve deliberate attention to the details of a text, but it also includes the effortless kind of reading described by avid or ludic readers. In both cases, the reader's psychological resources are denied to distraction, fully engaging mind and feelings in the text at hand.

The Librarian's Guide to Getting Lost

Children never question the value of fiction. It is a tragedy when adults become too practical to enjoy it. It is not real, they declare. Does it matter if it is real? We do not insist that music be real. A fictional work provides a sand box for imagining other identities and choices. Unhinging from our daily concerns often helps us to visualize new solutions to old problems, but that is not its only merit. The opportunity to step out of one's own skin and ride the imagination is a first-order pleasure, a cardinal delight.

Non-fiction can also help us see the world in a new way, but fiction has a particular importance to our psychological development. Birkets (1994) observes that "non-fiction has an authorial voice but fiction proposes a self" (92). Children can use fiction as a testing ground for their future selves. Is there any reason to stop this process when we reach adulthood? It is sad and a bit creepy to watch those adults who cease to imagine. It is as if their inner landscape is withering. Especially when adult life is at its most dreary, we may nurture a barely conscious idea of how life could be different. Imagine discovering a book that expresses just that idea. It would be irresistible to read, a sort of bibliotherapy to help one fight another day. Reading fiction may be just the therapy required to continue healthy maturation through all the years of our lives.

Unlike a map that helps us find our way in the real world, fiction helps us when our current course is unsatisfactory and we need to lose our way, at least for a time. It might be difficult to find the right reading material for such a journey. The average librarian is trained in the "read-alike" method of matching past choices to similar ones that have not been read yet. A "read-disalike" method might be required since old patterns may not be helpful when cutting a new path. What we seek may be difficult to articulate. Librarians are intent on findability, but this is better suited to non-fiction with its table of contents at the front and index at the back.

I can imagine a new reference work entitled, *A Librarian's Guide to Getting Lost*. Chapter one would lead librarians along the lines of Manguel's (2006) observance that the tidy ordering of libraries only seems to resist entropy, but wandering among the labyrinth shelves, one finds the complex order finally submitting to a sense of confusion. Chapter two would recommend abandoning Ranganathan's fourth law of library science, calling for the librarian to save the time of the reader. It is better to slow down to find the right book in this situation. Subsequent chapters would discuss Rosenblatt's transactional theory which explains how a text changes given the past experience and current context of the reader, and Ross' (1999) view that readers are engaged in a pursuit of meaning. Condon (2007) reviews both authorities and recommends improved library services. He advises away from the growing over-reliance on digital information discovery tools to the detriment of knowledge about the act of reading, and favours techniques that query more deeply into the experience of the reader. Before this imagined reference work concluded, librarians will have been taught the tracking skills of seasoned used bookstore browsers, including heightened sensitivity to clues left by others and to serendipity, with the end of helping patrons successfully find what they were not expecting.

Bibliotherapy

In the movie, *Stranger than Fiction* (Forster, 2007), the narrator concludes with a lesson that fiction is not merely an accessory to our lives, but sometimes is there to save our lives. Slow reading has been characterized as an activity that deeply engages the psyche, and as such it is an access point for people dealing with day-to-day problems as well as complex mental health issues. Using books to help people cope is called bibliotherapy, and it is a largely unspoken function of the librarian. Providing access to self-help books is one clear way in which the librarian performs this function, but there are more subtle forms that connect to the slow reading discussion of fiction. Gold (1990) suggests that imagery is one of the common powerful factors used in both fiction and psychotherapy, but that fiction has been largely untapped as a form of treatment.

The idea of bibliotherapy is not new. The reading of the Bible and other religious materials as therapy began in hospitals in North America in 1811 (Gold, 1990). In the 1930s, librarians worked with counsellors to prescribe literature for people experiencing problems (Pardeck, 1994), and social workers today have defined methods for using books in their practice (Pardeck, 1998). The library of a mental health institution may also provide indirect help through doctors or direct help to patients who visit the library.

The American Library Association recognizes that bibliotherapy is a special form of reader's advisory (ALA, 2008a) and lists professional resources (ALA, 2008b) but it is not part of library school training and not widely practiced. It is timely for librarians to consider their role in the psychological well-being of their community. One of the most productive ways forward will be collaborations between professional therapists and librarians. There are benefits in both directions. The therapist has the training in professional ethics and counselling, while the library is an ideal environment for reaching out to people in need who would never consider traditional therapeutic services, or be able to afford them. Together they could facilitate a discussion group for a target audience.

The Neuroscience of Slow Reading

This chapter on psychology has taken a look inside the mind to better understand the nature of slow reading. Controlled studies have shown that a slower reading rate is often a deliberate strategy to increase comprehension. Slow reading as deep engagement of the faculties can be viewed as an alternate state of consciousness, and fiction often best facilitates that process, sometimes to therapeutic ends. This material makes a case that slowness in its varied meanings places an important role in the reading experience. Studies in neuroscience reinforce that view.

It has been stated that the view of a reader as someone lost in a book is not just a stereotype. Johnson et al (1999) mapped differences in brain activity for the personality dimension of introversion and extraversion. At the one end of the dimension are extraverts, described as "gregarious, socially active, cheerful, assertive, and easily excitable". At the other end are introverts, tending toward reclusion and "preferring books" to other people. The brain activity of introverts was found to be associated with increased blood flow in the frontal lobes and the anterior thalamus. Using this research, Laney (2002) explained that introverts have more blood flow to the brain; it follows a different path and engages parts of the brain involved with remembering, problem solving, and planning. This explanation suggests that introverts -- the ones who prefer reading -- have a proclivity toward deeper neural activity that naturally slows down their overall responsiveness.

More evidence along these lines is provided by Wolf (2007) who observes that reading is an unnatural activity for humans. We were not born with genes for reading, but have repurposed neural circuitry to allow for it. Reading takes work for most people, and it is very difficult for others. Dyslexia is a common cause of involuntary slow reading. Interestingly, dyslexia has a greater than chance association with increased creativity, including geniuses like Edison, Da-Vinci, Einstein, and accomplished performers such as Keira

Knightley, Whoopi Goldberg and Johnny Depp. What would be lost if we could simply fix dyslexia with surgery or force brains to read faster using technology? The answer is not known, but Wolf makes the critical point that different styles of reading are instructive in gaining a broader understanding of how all of us read. We should not be too quick to label slowness as a negative thing. Perhaps evolution will make us faster readers, but Wolf disagrees with futurists like Kurzweil who think that acceleration is always positive:

> In music, in poetry, and in life, the rest, the pause, the slow movements are essential to comprehending the whole. Indeed, there are "delay neurons" whose sole function is to slow neuronal transmission by other neurons for milliseconds (213-214).

Our brains have evolved to use slowness as part of our overall information processing experience. This pattern points to a more fundamental design found throughout creation, the constant alternation from a thing to its opposite, yin-yang fashion, be that sowing and reaping, kingdoms rising and falling, or the universe expanding then contracting. As fast as our minds become, ultimately slowness may be required to make the most of reading.

This chapter has taken a psychological perspective, examining the "inner" phenomena associated with slow reading. This line of thinking might inadvertently reinforce a stereotype of readers as socially reclusive. The evidence shows the opposite. Two studies by the National Endowment for the Arts (NEA) found that literary readers are more likely to participate in social and civic events (2007, 2004). It is really not all that surprising. The first recorded tale, *The Epic of Gilgamesh*, is the story of the discovery of "Other" in a symbolic sense. It has been said that reading is thinking with the mind of another. Slow readers have a particular capacity to open up to new ideas, and allow the sense of self to be transformed. If the reader sought a book to escape the world, that book may contain the necessary artistic expression to facilitate a change in the reader, better equipping him or her for the world.

Chapter 5
The Practice of Slow Reading

Slow reading can be defined as practices that reduce the rate of reading to increase comprehension and pleasure. It is also much more than that. It should be clear by now that while slow reading often involves reducing the rate of reading, it also refers to any type of reading that more fully engages the faculties of the reader. This book has listed many such practices, from close reading of literary works and performance reading in the classroom, from booting down the computer and losing a few hours to a good book to seeking out local stories and authors. Still, not everything counts as slow reading, and a well-formed concept deserves an expression both of what it is, and what it is not. To that end, this book concludes by offering some practical suggestions regarding the practice of slow reading.

Select a Suitable Title for Slow Reading

Selecting a book can be a difficult choice. I have found good titles using online tools including Amazon's "also-bought" recommendations based on the purchases of others. The weakness of tools like these is the assumption that the reader wants more of the same. A better choice might be facilitated by a librarian trained in Reader's Advisory, though in my experience, librarians will also often start by trying to find titles similar to what the reader has previously enjoyed. I suggest that slow reading is facilitated by titles that are dissimilar to what the reader has read before, and ones that challenge the reader in unexpected ways. I am still working up the courage to read Dawkins' (2006), *The God Delusion*. On the other hand, rereading a title after several years has been known to offer an unanticipated vertigo of maturity, usually without regret. The choice is a personal one, highly dependent on the reader's current state. One need not feel compelled to read the classics, though *Paradise Lost* will slow you down. A trashy novel might express just what is needed by the reader. Recall too that reading local stories or stories by local authors are types of slow reading. You will know you have made a good choice if you feel a sense of anticipation about the book in your hands.

When it comes to the format of the title, a print book is generally preferable for slow reading. The web favours scanning and link surfing whereas the fixity of print encourages deep and sustained engagement in reading. In one case, I selected a title that was only available as an e-book. I reluctantly printed the book, though I used optimized print settings to allow for multiple pages on both sides of the paper. An audio book format can be a good choice because the pace is set by the narrator and the story is told in a continuous, linear style. A reader might follow along in the print book as the audio book is playing. Reading aloud to one another is an intimate experience.

Prepare for Reading

Fast food consumers do not prepare to eat; it does not matter what they wear and they already know the menu choices and prices. Fast reading is not much different. There is value in preparing for slow reading. Choose a setting that suits the content. A library is a better choice than a donut shop because the library does not post a time limit for your visit. Turn off the iPod. Research can give you a context to the book. Consider why you are reading this book. What do you hope to gain? Notice the selection of binding, paper and type. Was it picked for a reason? Now you are ready for slow reading.

Gear Down and Go Interior

Slow reading can be undertaken in many ways but all of them bring more of the reader's inner being into the act of reading. My personal practice involves reading at a moderate pace, usually in short spells, stopping when I notice that I am beginning to skip words. As I read, I occasionally stop to make notes that will later become part of a book review at my website. While I enjoy having people read and comment on my book reviews, it does not really matter in the end. The act of writing a review is itself helpful to me as a way of deepening my understanding of a book, committing it to memory, and bringing closure to it. Others may find note-taking too much of a distraction.

Read the entire book, jacket and preface, footnotes and appendices. Savour the illustrations and do not dare to skip the poetry. Subvocalize the words or read them aloud. Go back and reread passages. Argue with your book. How does it measure with your experience? Any deliberate choice that slows you down is adding to the richness of your reading. Be prepared for a figure-ground reversal as your setting fades into the background and you lose yourself in that effortless state of ludic reading. By opening your inner self to a book in this way, you invite ideas and feelings that enrich and expand your own interiority. Reading is the making of a deeper self.

Conclusion

It is often said that a person can only read about five thousand books in a lifetime. It is a small range of books given the accelerating quantity available to us. This limitation might lead some readers to rush their reading, thereby increasing the number of books. This response turns a reader into a tourist, jumping from experience to experience, noting only the highlights, being able to say he or she has done it, though not entirely sure what was done. Another response is to simply and happily acknowledge that life is indeed short, and that our smaller selection of books represents a unique expression of our character. This second choice removes the needless pressure from reading, and restores it as a great pleasure.

References

ALA (2008a). Using books to help patrons and bbliotherapy. Retrieved from http://wikis.ala.org/professionaltips/index.php/Using_Books_to_Help_Patrons_and_Bibliotherapy.

ALA (2008b). Bibliotherapy. Retrieved from http://wikis.ala.org/professionaltips/index.php/Bibliotherapy.

Amazon (2008a). Amazon Windowshop beta. Retrieved from http://www.windowshop.com/.

Amazon (2008b). Zoomii.com – The "real" online bookstore. Retrieved from http://zoomii.com.

Asimov, I. (1969). *Opus 100*. Boston: Houghton Mifflin.

Association of American Publishers (2008). AAP reports book sales rose to $ 25 billion in 2007. Retrieved from http://www.publishers.org/main/IndustryStats/indStats_02.htm.

Bacon, F. (2001). Essays, civil and moral. Vol. III, Part 1. *The Harvard classics*. NY: P.F. Collier & Son.

Baron, N. S. (2005). The future of written culture: Envisioning language in the New Millennium. Ibérica, *9*, 7-31. Retrieved from http://www.aelfe.org/documents/02-Ib9-Baron.pdf.

Bezos, J. (2007, November 26). The future of reading. *Newsweek.* Retrieved from http://www.newsweek.com/id/70983/page/1.

Birkets, S. (1994). *The Gutenberg elegies: The fate of reading in an electronic age.* Boston: Faber and Faber.

Carr, N. (2008). Is Google making us stupid? *Altantic,* July/August. Retrieved from http://www.theatlantic.com/doc/200807/google.

Carver, R. P. (1990). *Reading rate: A review of research and theory.* San Diego, CA: Academic Press.

Condon, S. (2007) The Reader and the librarian. *Proceedings Washington Library Association Conference 2007,* Kennewick, WA. Retrieved from http://dlist.sir.arizona.edu/2007/.

Chen, N., Guimbretiere, F., Dixon, M. et al (2008). Navigation techniques for dual-display e-book readers. CHI 2008. Retrieved from http://www.cs.umd.edu/~francois/Papers/EBookReaderCHI08.pdf.

Cohen, N. (2008, April 23). A slice of German Wikipedia to be captured on paper. *The New York Times.* Retrieved from http://www.nytimes.com/2008/04/23/business/media/23wiki.html.

Darbyshire, P. (2007). Please: A novel. Retrieved from http://peterdarbyshire.com/please.html.

Dawkins, R. (2006). *The God delusion*. Boston, MA: Houghton Mifflin Co.

De Rosa, C., Cantrell, J., Cellentani, D., Hawk, J., Jenkins, L., and Wilson, A. (2005). *Perceptions of libraries and information resources: A report to the OCLC membership*. Retrieved from http://www.oclc.org/reports/pdfs/Percept_all.pdf.

Donahue, P.L., Daane, M.C., and Jin, Y. (2005). *The nation's report card: Reading 2003 (NCES 2005–453)*. U.S. Department of Education, Institute of Education Sciences, National Center for Education Statistics. Washington, DC: U.S. Government Printing Office. Retrieved from http://nces.ed.gov/nationsreportcard/pdf/main2003/2005453.pdf.

Duke, C. R. (1982). *Literature and the making of meaning*. Murray, Kentucky: Department of English, Murray State University.

Dupuy, B., & McQuillan, J. (1997). Handcrafted books: Check this out! *Canadian Modern Language Review*, *53*(4), p. 743.

Dillon, A. (1992) Reading from paper versus screens: A critical review of the empirical literature. *Ergonomics*, *35*(10), 1297-1326.

Doctorow, C. (2006). About Cory Doctorow. Retrieved from http://craphound.com/bio.php.

Elder, L. & Paul, R. (2004). Critical thinking ... and the art of close reading, Part IV. *Journal of Developmental Education, 28*(2), 36-37.

Faust, M. A. & Glenzer, N. (2000). "I could read those parts over and over": Eighth graders rereading to enhance enjoyment and learning with literature. *Journal of Adolescent & Adult Literacy, 44*(3), 234-239.

Forster, M. (2007). *Stranger than fiction.* Sony Pictures Home Entertainment.

Frank, S. D. (1992). *Remember everything you read: The Evelyn Wood 7-Day speed reading & learning program.* Avon.

Gainman, N. (2008). The results of free. Retrieved from http://journal.neilgaiman.com/2008/07/results-of-free.html.

Galef, D. (1998). *Second thoughts: A focus on rereading.* Detroit, MI: Wayne State University Press.

Gates, B. (1995). *The road ahead.* New York: Viking.

Gold, J. (1990). *Read for your life: Literature as a life support system.* Markham, Ont: Fitzhenry & Whiteside.

Gomez, J. (2008). *Print is dead: Books in our digital age.* London: Macmillan.

Greek, M. (cited in Miller, 2008, August 15). LJ's movers & shakers strategize about how to secure a vital future. *Library Journal.* Retrieved from http://www.libraryjournal.com/article/CA6585850.html.

Grimes, W. (2006, September 22) You're a slow reader? Congratulations. *The New York Times*, p. 25.

Haggith, M. (2008). *Paper trails: From trees to trash - the true cost of paper*. Virgin Books.

Harris, M. H. (1998). *Into the Future: The foundation of library and information services in the post-industrial era*, Contemporary studies in information management, policy, and services (2nd ed). Greenwich, Conn: Ablex Pub.

Honoré, C. (2007). Slowing down in a world built for speed. *TED: Ideas worth spreading*. Retrieved from http://www.ted.com/index.php/talks/carl_honore_praises_slowness.html.

Honoré, C. (2004). *In praise of slow: How a worldwide movement is changing the cult of speed*. Vintage Canada.

Hyönä, J. & Nurminen, A. (2006). Do adult readers know how they read? Evidence from eye movement patterns and verbal reports. *British Journal of Psychology*, *1*(97), 31-50.

Jarvis, J. (2008). Apologizing for the book. Retrieved from http://www.buzzmachine.com/2008/07/23/apologizing-for-the-book/.

Johnson, D. L., Wiebe, J. S., Gold, S. M., Andreasen, N. C., et al. (1999). Cerebral blood flow and personality: A positron emission tomography study. *The American Journal of Psychiatry*, *156*(2), 252-257.

Kelley, T. P. (1994). *The black Donnellys*. Firefly.

Kirschenbaum, M. (2007, December). How reading is being reimagined. *The Chronicle of Higher Education*, *54*(15).

Kozak, G. (2003). Printed scholarly books and e-book reading devices: A comparative life cycle assessment of two book options. University of Michigan, Center for Sustainable Systems. Retrieved from http://css.snre.umich.edu/css_doc/CSS03-04.pdf.

Krashen, S. (2004). *The power of reading* (2nd ed.). Westport, Connecticut: Libraries Unlimited.

Kurzweil, R. (2005). *The singularity is near: When humans transcend biology*. New York: Viking.

Laney, M. O. (2002). *The introvert advantage: How to thrive in an extrovert world*. Workman.

Lee, G. S. (1907). *The lost art of reading*. New York: G. P. Putnam's sons.

Lessig, L. (2004). *Free culture: How big media uses technology and the law to lock down culture and control creativity*. New York: Penguin Press.

Levy, D. M. (2001). Reading and attention. Chapter 6 in *Scrolling forward: Making sense of documents in the digital age* (110 – 117). NY: Arcade.

Lindblom, K. (2005). Close reading on your feet: Performance in the English language arts classroom. *English Journal*, 95(1), 116-119.

Lyons, C. (2007). The library: A distinct local voice? *First Monday, 12*(3). Retrieved from http://firstmonday.org/htbin/cgiwrap/bin/ojs/index.php/fm/issue/view/225.

Manguel, A. (2006). *The library at night* (1st ed.). Toronto: A.A. Knopf Canada.

Metzger, M. (1998). *Teaching reading*. Phi Delta Kappan, *80*(3), 240-246.

Miall, D. S. & Kuiken, D. (2002). A feeling for fiction: becoming what we behold. *Poetics, 30*(4), 221–241.

Moberg, A., Johansson, M., Finnveden, G. & Jonsson, A. (2007). Screening environmental lifecycle assessment of printed, web based and table e-paper newspaper. Stockholm: Centre for Sustainable Communications. Retrieved from http://www.csc.kth.se/sustain/publications/reportfiles/Report%20e-paper_final.pdf.

Morville, P. (2005). *Ambient findability*. Sebastopol, Calif: O'Reilly.

Murray, H. (1991). Close reading, closed writing. *College English, 53*(2), 195.

Nardi, B. and O'Day, V. (1999) *Information ecologies: Using technology with heart*. Cambridge, Mass: MIT Press.

National Endowment for the Arts (2007). *To read or not to read*. Retrieved from http://www.nea.gov/research/toread.pdf.

National Endowment for the Arts (2004). *Reading at risk.* Retrieved from http://www.nea.gov/pub/ReadingAtRisk.pdf.

Nell, V. (1988). *Lost in a book: The psychology of reading for pleasure* (p. 336). New Haven [Conn.]: Yale University Press.

Nicoll, W. R. (1904). *The lost art of reading.* New York: T. Y. Crowell & Co.

Nielsen, J. (2007). Long vs. short articles as content strategy. *Alertbox.* Retrieved from http://www.useit.com/alertbox/content-strategy.html.

Nielsen, J. (1997). How users read on the Web. *Alertbox.* Retrieved from http://www.useit.com/alertbox/9710a.html.

Nietzsche, F. (1997). *Daybreak: Thoughts on the prejudices of morality.* Maudemarie Clark (editor), R.J. Hollingdale (translator). NY: Cambridge University Press.

Oder, N. (2008, February 7). Is it OK for a library to lend a Kindle? *Library Journal.* Retrieved from http://www.libraryjournal.com/article/CA6530211.html.

Oz, A. (1999). Excerpt from the book *The story begins: Essays on literature. Nation, 268*(22), 13-14.

Pardeck, J. T. (1998). *Children in foster care and adoption: A guide to bibliotherapy* (p. 103). Westport, Conn: Greenwood.

Pardeck, J. T. (1994). Using literature to help adolescents cope with problems. *Adolescence, 29*(114), 421-427.

Penn, M., & Zalesne, E. K. (2007). *Microtrends: The small forces behind tomorrow's big changes.* Twelve.

Peterson, E. H. (2006). *Eat this book: A conversation in the art of spiritual reading.* Grand Rapids, Michigan: William B. Eerdmans.

Piddington, S. (1973, June). The special joys of super-slow reading. *Reader's Digest, 102*(614).

Pike, M. A. (2004). 'Well-being' through reading: Drawing upon literature and literacy in spiritual education. *International Journal of Children's Spirituality, 9*(2), 155-162.

Postman, N. (1986). *Amusing ourselves to death: Public discourse in the age of show business.* New York, N.Y., U.S.A: Penguin Books.

Prose, F. (2006). *Reading like a writer.* NY: HarperCollins.

Pulp & Paper International (2000, July). San Francisco, Calif: Miller Freeman Publications.

Redekop, C. (2007). *Shelf monkey.* Toronto: ECW Press.

Rosenblatt, L. M. (1994). *The reader, the text, the poem: The transactional theory of the literary work.* Carbondale: Southern Illinois University Press.

Ross, C. S., McKechnie, L. (E.F.) & Rothbauer, P. M. (2006). *Reading matters: What the research reveals about reading, libraries, and community*. Westport, CT: Libraries Unlimited.

Ross, C. S. (1999). Finding without seeking: the information encounter in the context of reading for pleasure. *Information Processing and Management, 35*(6), 783-799.

Schwartz, J. (2005). Let's change this. *Jonathan Swartz's Blog*. Retrieved from http://blogs.sun.com/jonathan/entry/let_s_change_this.

Schwartz, L. S. (1996). *Ruined by reading: A life in books*. Beacon Press.

Sellen, A. J., & Harper, R. H. R. (2001). *The myth of the paperless office* (1st ed.). The MIT Press.

Shillingsburg, P. L. (2006). *From Gutenberg to Google: Electronic representations of literary texts*. Cambridge, UK: Cambridge University Press.

Sire, J. (1978). *How to read slowly: A Christian guide to reading with the mind*. Downers Grove, IL: InterVarsity Press.

Slow Food (2008). Good, clean and fair food. Retrieved from http://www.slowfood.com/.

Slow Food (2008). Our philosophy. Retrieved from http://www.slowfood.com/about_us/eng/philosophy.lasso.

Smith, A. & MacKinnon, J.B. (2007). *The 100-Mile diet: A year of eating locally.* Toronto: Vintage.

Smith, D. I. (2004). The poet, the child and the blackbird: Aesthetic reading and spiritual development. *International Journal of Children's Spirituality*, *9*(2), 143-154.

Sutherland, J. (2006). *How to read a novel: A user's guide.* NY: St. Martin's.

Waters, L. (2007). Time for reading, *Chronicle of Higher Education*, *53*(23).

Weinreich, H., Obendorf, H., Herder, E. & Mayer, M. (2008). Not quite the average: An empirical study of web use. *ACM Transactions on the web*, *2*(1).

Williams, J. J. (2005). Culture and policy: An interview with Mark Bauerlein. *Minnesota Review*, *63/64*, 159-177.

Wolf, M. (2007). *Proust and the squid: The story and science of the reading brain.* NY: HarperCollins.

World Resources Institute (1998). Global environmental trends: Production and consumption. Retrieved from http://www.wri.org/publication/content/8440.

Index

About the Author

John Miedema is an IT Specialist with IBM where he specializes in web technologies. He is a part-time student in the Master of Library and Information Science program at the University of Western Ontario, with interests in reading research and open source for libraries. John lives with his wife and two teenagers in Southwestern Ontario.

CPSIA information can be obtained at www.ICGtesting.com
Printed in the USA
LVOW04s2032171114

414097LV00003B/340/P